Let it Happen

Mission: To Proclaim Transformation and Truth

Publisher: Transformed Publishing, Cocoa, FL

Website: www.transformedpublishing.com

Email: transformedpublishing@gmail.com

ISBN: 978-1-953241-77-1 (paperback)

ISBN: 978-1-953241-70-2 (Ebook)

Let it Happen

DIANA ROBINSON

Dedication

To each person who makes the investment of their time to read this book and listen for the Voice behind the voice.

May your reluctancy be replaced with zeal to maximize your God-given gifts, talents, and purpose.

But all things become visible when they are exposed by the light [of God's precepts], for it is light that makes everything visible. For this reason He says,

"Awake, sleeper,
And arise from the dead,
And Christ will shine [as dawn] upon you *and* give you light."

Therefore see that you walk carefully [living life with honor, purpose, and courage; shunning those who tolerate and enable evil], not as the unwise, but as wise [sensible, intelligent, discerning people], making the very most of your time [on earth, recognizing and taking advantage of each opportunity and using it with wisdom and diligence], because the days are [filled with] evil. Therefore do not be foolish *and* thoughtless, but understand *and* firmly grasp what the will of the Lord is.

-Ephesians 5:13-17 AMP

Table of Contents

Journaling space for you to plan, pursue, & record your progress.

Purpose

"If only they would live up to their potential," a classic statement people make when pondering why someone who *could* do better, *won't* do better.

How can an onlooker, from the exterior, see something so great *inside* another person that the person themselves fails to even notice or acknowledge?

Let's break down the word *potential*.

> **Potent**[1] – having or wielding force, authority, or influence: powerful
>
> **-ial**[2] (suffix) – adds 'relating to' the root word

As stated, let's conclude that we operate in our potential when we relate to the readily available and effective force, authority, influence, and power God has prepackaged within us.

When a smell or taste dominates our physical senses, we may say, "Oh, that's potent," meaning something is standing out more powerfully than everything else that is present, including other things in the environment also engaging our senses.

We are each potently filled with gifts, talents, and purpose. We must *actively* relate to them. *What does that mean?* We must prioritize, practice, and perfect our intentionally given God-allotted assets within us.

---

[1] "Potent." Merriam-Webster.com Dictionary, Merriam-Webster, https://www.merriam-webster.com /dictionary/potent. Accessed 21 Dec. 2023.
[2] Dictionary.com unabridged based on the Random House Unabridged Dictionary ©Random House. INC. 2023. Accessed 21 Dec. 2023

A seed contains all the things needed for life. The difference between a dormant seed and a producing seed is its location. A seed never sown, is full of potential, yet unproductive. A seed, able to grow to maturity, produce fruit, and replenish itself, demonstrates the power of the Creator's design.

The seed is all sufficient within itself but must go through a process not visible to others while it is isolated in the ground with the pressure of the earth sealed on top of it and the light on the other side of the weight. Over time, the seed germinates, winning the fight to get out of its own casing (self-limitation). Then it strengthens and pushes past the adversity of the soil (the same soil it *needs* to grow) breaking through to the light.

When we allow seeds (gifts, talents, and purpose) to sit bagged on the *shelf of life*, we stop the growth process from even beginning.

> For out of His fullness [the superabundance of His grace and truth] we have all received grace upon grace [spiritual blessing upon spiritual blessing, favor upon favor, and gift heaped upon gift].
>
> -John 1:16 AMP

Gift heaped upon gift. What a potent statement. As we begin to operate in our gifting, we find other gifts heaped upon more gifts. Once we get a hold of this truth, we will stop coveting other people's gifts and cultivate our own gifts.

Seed packages contain directions. When to plant, where to plant, spacing and depth specifications, and the optimum amount of sunlight and water recommendations, which are all unique to the seed.

When: There is a set time when there will be a great demand for the solutions to the problems of life your gifts, talents, and purpose manifest. As that time approaches, we are to become efficient and excellent in our niche of life to maximize our effectiveness.

> And it came to pass, when Joshua was by Jericho, that he lifted his eyes and looked, and behold, a Man stood opposite him with His sword drawn in His hand. And Joshua went to Him and said to Him, "*Are* You for us or for our adversaries?" So He said, "No, but *as* Commander of the army of the Lord I have now come." And Joshua fell on his face to the earth and worshiped, and said to Him, "What does my Lord say to His servant?" Then the Commander of the Lord's army said to Joshua, "Take your sandal off your foot, for the place where you stand is holy." And Joshua did so.

-Joshua 5:13-15

As Commander of the army of the Lord I have now come, Joshua spent decades of preparation; holding on to the truth of the promise, studying the word of God, serving Moses faithfully, and being constructed by God into a leader, to arrive at *this* place. To move into the acquisition of the promised land, firmly positioned in unison with the Commander of the army of the Lord.

Where: There is a profitable place for you. While the laws, statutes, and commands of God are for all, the *precepts* of God are individualized. The precepts are the predetermined steps, prior to your conception, for you to walk in. Find the place where your foot fits, and you will profit.

Physically, when we put on someone else's worn shoes, even if they are the same size we wear, they do not fit the same. The impact of the walk and weight of the other person is different, bringing unique change to the form. It becomes apparent after taking a few steps. This applies to *precepts*. What is for you is for you, what is for me is for me, what is for them is for them. As my pastor, Errol Beckford says, "Something may sound good, and be neither sound nor good for you!" Below are some verses from Psalm 119 to explore and emphasize the importance and benefits of walking in His precepts for your life. After all, it is Him who sent you into the earth on purpose, for a purpose. There is a purpose in every promise and a promise in every purpose.

vs. 4 You have commanded *us* to keep Your precepts diligently.

vs. 15 I will meditate on Your precepts, and contemplate Your ways.

vs. 27-28 Make me understand the way of Your precepts; so shall I meditate on Your wonderful works. My soul melts from heaviness; strengthen me according to Your word.

vs. 40 Behold, I long for Your precepts; revive me in Your righteousness.

vs. 45 And I will walk at liberty, for I seek Your precepts.

vs. 56 This has become mine, because I kept Your precepts.

vs. 69 The proud have forged a lie against me, *but* I will keep Your precepts with *my* whole heart.

vs. 87 They almost made an end of me on earth, but I did not forsake Your precepts.

vs. 93 I will never forget Your precepts, for by them You have given me life.

vs. 94 I *am* Yours, save me; for I have sought Your precepts.

vs. 100 I understand more than the ancients, because I keep Your precepts.

vs. 104 Through Your precepts I get understanding; therefore I hate every false way.

vs. 110 The wicked have laid a snare for me, yet I have not strayed from Your precepts.

vs. 128 Therefore all *Your* precepts *concerning* all *things* I consider to *be* right; I hate every false way.

vs. 134 Redeem me from the oppression of man, that I may keep Your precepts.

vs. 141 I *am* small and despised, *yet* I do not forget Your precepts.

vs. 159 Consider how I love Your precepts; revive me, O Lord, according to Your lovingkindness.

vs. 168 I keep Your precepts and Your testimonies, for all my ways *are* before You.

vs. 173 Let Your hand become my help, for I have chosen Your precepts.

Spacing & Depth: A specific distance must be left between seeds to allow for future growth and fruition. Contrary to the opinion of most people, being separated from the majority is beneficial and purposeful for a productive future. There is no need to compete for resources in *one* space when we have endless opportunities to explore before us, that are already reserved for us. We must not be intimidated by self-imposed limitations or current circumstances and learn to enter into the rest of submission. Submission, coming under the mission of God for our lives, becoming fully convinced, "The things which are impossible with men are possible with God" (*see* Luke 18:27).

> I returned and saw under the sun that—the race is not to the swift, nor the battle to the strong, nor bread to the wise, nor riches to men of understanding, nor favor to men of skill; but time and chance happen to them all.
>
> -Ecclesiastes 9:11

. . . 'Not by might nor by power, but by My Spirit,' says the Lord of hosts.

-Zechariah 4:6

The enemy works to deceive us and separate us from God in our mind. He wants us to feel as if we are aliens and do not deserve the prosperity God has put before us to 'tend and to keep' (*see* Genesis 2:15).

And you, who once were alienated and enemies in your mind by wicked works, yet now He has reconciled in the body of His flesh through death, to present you holy, and blameless, and above reproach in His sight—if indeed you continue in the faith, grounded and steadfast, and are not moved away from the hope of the gospel which you heard, which was preached to every creature under heaven, of which I, Paul, became a minister.

-Colossians 1:21-23

The truth is, we are ambassadors and *not* aliens. An ambassador has full authority and the backing and resources of their homeland.

Now then, we are ambassadors for Christ, as though God were pleading through us: we implore you on Christ's behalf, be reconciled to God.

-2 Corinthians 5:20

For our citizenship is in heaven, from which we also eagerly wait for the Savior, the Lord Jesus Christ,

-Philippians 3:20

An ideal planting depth is also stated on a seed package to ensure the *'to be'* root network will develop suitably to anchor the plant as it increases in size and gather the necessary nutrients to sustain *that* plant. Just like the root system being established in the hidden place, remember, *what you are doing when nobody is looking determines your level and value when you come into view.* Deep roots have access to hidden waters and shallow roots partake only of what is on the surface.

Sunlight & Water: What causes one plant to thrive can kill another. What is *right* depends on the design and intention of the Creator. There is a customized grace for every God-given assignment. His grace is freely poured out in His presence and in His presence, there is grace.

> "Blessed is the man who trusts in the Lord, and whose hope is the Lord. For he shall be like a tree planted by the waters, which spreads out its roots by the river, and will not fear when heat comes; but its leaf will be green, and will not be anxious in the year of drought, nor will cease from yielding fruit.["]

> -Jeremiah 17:7-8

Consider *who* and *what* principles you allow to light your way and water your path.

> Blessed is the man who walks not in the counsel of the ungodly, nor stands in the path of sinners, nor sits in the seat of the scornful; but his delight *is* in the law of the Lord, and in His law he meditates day and night. He shall be like a tree planted by the rivers of water, that brings forth its fruit in its season, whose leaf also shall not wither; and

whatever he does shall prosper. The ungodly are not so, but *are* like the chaff which the wind drives away. Therefore the ungodly shall not stand in the judgment, nor sinners in the congregation of the righteous. For the Lord knows the way of the righteous, but the way of the ungodly shall perish.

-Psalm 1

Then Moses said to the Lord, "See, You say to me, 'Bring up this people.' But You have not let me know whom You will send with me. Yet You have said, 'I know you by name, and you have also found grace in My sight.' Now therefore, I pray, if I have found grace in Your sight, show me now Your way, that I may know You and that I may find grace in Your sight. And consider that this nation *is* Your people." And He said, "My Presence will go *with you*, and I will give you rest." Then he said to Him, "If Your Presence does not go *with us*, do not bring us up from here. For how then will it be known that Your people and I have found grace in Your sight, except You go with us? So we shall be separate, Your people and I, from all the people who *are* upon the face of the earth." So the Lord said to Moses, "I will also do this thing that you have spoken; for you have found grace in My sight, and I know you by name."

-Exodus 33:12-17

Let us therefore come boldly to the throne of grace, that we may obtain mercy and find grace to help in time of need.

-Hebrews 4:16

Shame, despair, and inadequacy say 'we have to get right before we can come to God' but Hebrews 4:16 clearly states, "Let us therefore come boldly to the throne of grace, that we may obtain mercy and find grace to help in time of need"- to reemphasize again, *in our time of need.*

We use tools in everyday life to care for our yards, cook, clean, construct hobbies, make repairs, etc. We know it would be extremely difficult, if not impossible, to venture into these tasks without the right provisions.

God has the provisions necessary to care for us, fulfill us, cleanse us, construct us, and repair us. We must come to Him first.

In the beginning God . . .

-Genesis 1:1

Introduction

More often than we recognize, we interfere with and delay the manifestation of the desires of our hearts.

> **let**[1] – (v.) to cause to: make
> to give opportunity to or fail to prevent
> to free from or as if from confinement
> to permit to enter, pass, or leave

Throughout the first chapter of Genesis, God created the heavens and the earth. Each declaration He made began with the word, *Let!*

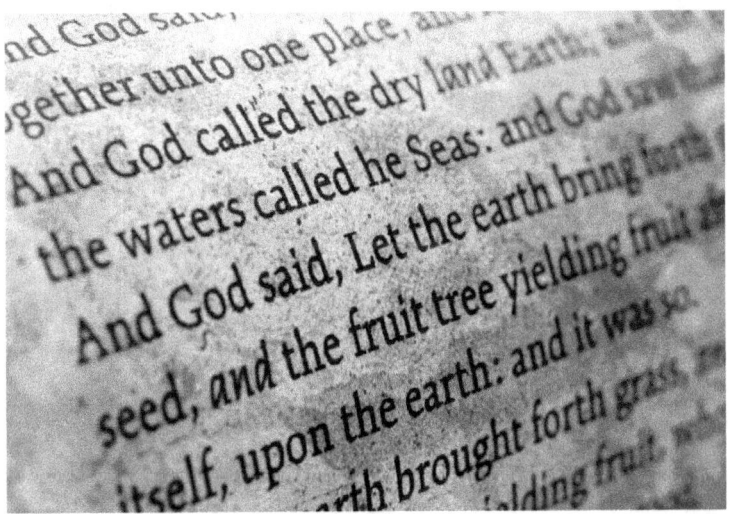

A declaration is a formal announcement of a decree. A decree is an official order issued by an authority. Therefore, the declaration is verbally executing and enforcing something that was *all-ready* established.

[1]"Let." Merriam-Webster.com Dictionary, Merriam-Webster, https://www.merriam-webster.com /dictionary/let. Accessed 21 Dec. 2023.

Day 1: Then God said, "Let there be light"; and there was light. -Genesis 1:3

Day 2: Then God said, "Let there be a firmament in the midst of the waters and let it divide the waters from the waters." -Genesis 1:6

Day 3: Then God said, "Let the waters under the heavens be gathered together into one place and let dry *land* appear"; and it was so. -Genesis 1:9

Then God said, "Let the earth bring forth grass, the herb that yield seed, *and* the fruit tree that yields fruit according to its kind, whose seed is in itself, on the earth"; and it was so. -Genesis 1:11

Day 4: Then God said, "Let there be lights in the firmament of the heavens to divide the day from the night; and let them be for signs and seasons, and for days and years; and let them be for lights in the firmament of the heavens to give light on the earth"; and it was so. –Genesis 1:14-15

Day 5: Then God said, "Let the waters abound with an abundance of living creatures, and let birds fly above the earth across the face of the firmament of the heavens." –Genesis 1:20

Day 6: Then God said, "Let the earth bring forth the living creature according to its kind: cattle and creeping thing and beast of the earth, *each* according to its kind"; and it was so. -Genesis 1:20

Then God said, "Let Us make man in Our image, according to Our likeness; let them have dominion over the fish of the sea, over the birds of the air, and over the cattle, over all the earth and over every creeping thing that creeps on the earth." -Genesis 1:26

Even when, "The earth was without form, and void; and darkness was on the face of the deep," the Spirit of God was hovering - in position, ready, anticipating, the verbal commanding declaration of, *Let* (*see* Genesis 1:2-3).

Let it Happen.

Let what is *all-ready* hovering in the Spirit be activated. Even when we can't make sense of a situation (when it is without form; beholding the result in the not yet recognizable future); when we feel empty, or *our* plans have been canceled (voided), and we face despair and destitution (darkness); the willing and available Spirit of God has all things ready.

> For we are His workmanship, created in Christ Jesus for good works, which God prepared beforehand that we should walk in them.
>
> -Ephesians 2:10

Let it be according to His word. You have been handcrafted by God, created in Christ Jesus for good works, to *do* all things that God already prepared beforehand that you *should* walk in them.

13

You did not choose Me, but I chose you and appointed you that you should go and bear fruit, and *that* your fruit should remain, that whatever you ask the Father in My name He may give you.

-John 15:16

We *should* go, we *should* bear fruit, and it *should* remain. The prepaid course is already measured, marked, and mapped. In vain, we worry, wonder, and grow weary toiling - trying to build the course. God already created the course, and wonderfully formed, uniquely crafted, and equipped each of us to bring to completion what He already wrote about us in His book.

Your eyes saw my substance, being yet unformed. And in Your book they all were written, the days fashioned for me, when *as yet there were* none of them.

-Psalm 139:16

During creation, God made everything needed to sustain life before He made man. Water, soil, and seed were undeniably created by God. Then He made man with God-given dominion to sow the seed into the soil and claim space to establish the purpose for which it was sent. For example, farmers designate specific ground and name the ground based on the seed that was sown there.

Each of us is filled with seed form gifts, talents, and purpose we are to sow into the earth, and water with the promises of His word, then let God give the increase.

I planted, Apollos watered, but God gave the increase. So then neither he who plants is anything, nor he who waters, but God who gives the increase. Now he who plants and he who waters are one, and each one will receive his own reward according to his own labor.

-1 Corinthians 3:6-8

As we prepare to move through the chapters of this book: *Resistance, Recompense, Reconciliation, Response, & Results,* we must establish one very important thing – you are not disqualified! In fact, you have been indefinitely qualified, verified by the opposition you have faced. This message is for you! Here is some Scriptural proof before we move any further:

If I ascend into heaven, You *are* there; If I make my bed in hell, behold, You *are there*.

-Psalm 139:8

Then Ananias answered, "Lord, I have heard from many about this man [Saul], how much harm he has done to Your saints in Jerusalem. And here he has authority from the chief priests to bind all who call on Your name." But the Lord said to him, "Go, for he is a chosen vessel of Mine to bear My name before Gentiles, kings, and the children of Israel.

-Acts 9:13-15

"Return, O backsliding children," says the Lord; "for I am married to you. I will take you, one from a city and two from a family, and I will bring you to Zion.

-Jeremiah 3:14

For God so loved the world that He gave His only begotten Son, that whoever believes in Him should not perish but have everlasting life. For God did not send His Son into the world to condemn the world, but that the world through Him might be saved.

-John 3:16-17

Who shall separate us from the love of Christ? Shall tribulation, or distress, or persecution, or famine, or nakedness, or peril, or sword?

-Romans 8:35-36

We love Him because He first loved us.

-1 John 4:19

The last chapter of this book, *Results* beginning on page 63 is journaling space for you to plan, pursue, & record your progress. Start now by recording a vision God has given you.

Let Scriptures Reference Section

These Scriptures were selected from the New Testament, with bold emphasis by the author, for you to reference and declare over your life as God ministers to you throughout the chapters of this book.

Let your light so shine before men, that they may see your good works and glorify your Father in heaven. -Matthew 5:16

Then Jesus said to the centurion, "Go your way; and as you have believed, *so* **let** it be done for you." And his servant was healed that same hour. -Matthew 8:13

Then He touched their eyes, saying, "According to your faith **let** it be to you."-Matthew 9:29

Then Jesus answered and said to her, "O woman, great is your faith! **Let** it be to you as you desire." And her daughter was healed from that very hour. -Matthew 15:28

"So then, they are no longer two but one flesh. Therefore what God has joined together, **let** not man separate." -Matthew 19:6

But Jesus said, "**Let** the little children come to Me, and do not forbid them; for of such is the kingdom of heaven." -Matthew 19:14

And He said to them, "He who has ears to hear, **let** him hear!" -Mark 4:9

Then Mary said, "Behold the maidservant of the Lord! **Let** it be to me according to your word." And the angel departed from her. -Luke 1:38

When He had stopped speaking, He said to Simon, "Launch out into the deep and **let** down your nets for a catch." -Luke 5:4

Now it happened, on a certain day, that He got into a boat with His disciples. And He said to them, "**Let** us cross over to the other side of the lake." And they launched out. -Luke 8:22

Then He said to *them* all, "If anyone desires to come after Me, **let** him deny himself, and take up his cross daily, and follow Me.["] -Luke 9:23

"**Let** not your heart be troubled; you believe in God, believe also in Me.["] -John 14:1

"Peace I leave with you, My peace I give to you; not as the world gives do I give to you. **Let** not your heart be troubled, neither **let** it be afraid." -John 14:27

"But that the world may know that I love the Father, and as the Father gave Me commandment, so I do. Arise, **let** us go from here." -John 14:31

Then Peter said to them, "Repent, and **let** every one of you be baptized in the name of Jesus Christ for the remission of sins; and you shall receive the gift of the Holy Spirit. -Acts 2:38

Therefore **let** it be known to you, brethren, that through this Man is preached to you the forgiveness of sins; -Acts 13:38

Then there arose a loud outcry. And the scribes of the Pharisees' party arose and protested, saying, "We find no evil in this man; but if a spirit or an angel has spoken to him, **let** us not fight against God." -Acts 23:9

Certainly not! Indeed, **let** God be true but every man a liar. As it is written: "That You may be justified in Your words, and may overcome when You are judged." -Romans 3:4

Therefore do not **let** sin reign in your mortal body, that you should obey it in its lusts. -Romans 6:12

Having then gifts differing according to the grace that is given to us, *let us use them*: if prophecy, *let us prophesy* in proportion to our faith; or ministry, *let us use it* in *our* ministering; he who teaches, in teaching; he who exhorts, in exhortation; he who gives, with liberality; he who leads, with diligence; he who shows mercy, with cheerfulness. *Let* love *be* without hypocrisy. Abhor what is evil. Cling to what is good. -Romans 12:6-9

Let every soul be subject to the governing authorities. For there is no authority except from God, and the authorities that exist are appointed by God. -Romans 13:1

The night is far spent, the day is at hand. Therefore **let** us cast off the works of darkness, and **let** us put on the armor of light. **Let** us walk properly, as in the day, not in revelry and drunkenness, not in lewdness and lust, not in strife and envy. -Romans 13:12-13

Therefore **let** us not judge one another anymore, but rather resolve this, not to put a stumbling block or a cause to fall in *our* brother's way. -Romans 14:13

Therefore do not **let** your good be spoken of as evil; -Romans 14:16

Therefore **let** us pursue the things *which make* for peace and the things by which one may edify another. -Romans 14:19

Let each of us please *his* neighbor for *his* good, leading to edification. -Romans 15:2

[T]hat, as it is written, "He who glories, **let** him glory in the Lord." -1 Corinthians 1:31

According to the grace of God which was given to me, as a wise master builder I have laid the foundation, and another builds on it. But **let** each one take heed how he builds on it. -1 Corinthians 3:10

Let no one deceive himself. If anyone among you seems to be wise in this age, **let** him become a fool that he may become wise. For the wisdom of this world is foolishness with God. For it is written, "He catches the wise in their *own* craftiness"; and again, "The Lord knows the thoughts of the wise, that they are futile." Therefore **let** no one boast in men. For all things are yours: whether Paul or Apollos or Cephas, or the world or life or death, or things present or things to come—all are yours. And you *are* Christ's, and Christ *is* God's. -1 Corinthians 3:18-23

Let a man so consider us, as servants of Christ and stewards of the mysteries of God. -1 Corinthians 4:1

Nevertheless, because of sexual immorality, **let** each man have his own wife, and **let** each woman have her own husband. -1 Corinthians 7:2

All things are lawful for me, but not all things are helpful; all things are lawful for me, but not all things edify. **Let** no one seek his own, but each one the other's *well-being*. -1 Corinthians 10:23-24

Even so you, since you are zealous for spiritual *gifts, let it be* for the edification of the church *that* you seek to excel. -1 Corinthians 14:12

Let all that you *do* be done with love. -1 Corinthians 16:14

Therefore, having these promises, beloved, **let** us cleanse ourselves from all filthiness of the flesh and spirit, perfecting holiness in the fear of God. -2 Corinthians 7:1

So **let** each one *give* as he purposes in his heart, not grudgingly or of necessity; for God loves a cheerful giver. -2 Corinthians 9:7

If we live in the Spirit, **let** us also walk in the Spirit. **Let** us not become conceited, provoking one another, envying one another. -Galatians 5:25-26

But **let** each one examine his own work, and then he will have rejoicing in himself alone, and not in another. For each one shall bear his own load. **Let** him who is taught the word share in all good things with him who teaches. Do not be deceived, God is not mocked; for whatever a man sows, that he will also reap. For he who sows to his flesh will of the flesh reap corruption, but he who sows to the Spirit will of the Spirit reap everlasting life. And **let** us not grow weary while doing good, for in due season we shall reap if we do not lose heart. Therefore, as we have opportunity, **let** us do good to all, especially to those who are of the household of faith. -Galatians 6:4-10

[A]nd be renewed in the spirit of your mind, and that you put on the new man which was created according to God, in true righteousness and holiness. Therefore, putting away lying, "*Let* each one *of you* speak truth with his neighbor," for we are members of one another. "Be angry, and do not sin": do not **let** the sun go down on your wrath, nor give place to the devil. **Let** him who stole steal no longer, but rather **let** him labor, working with *his* hands what is good, that he may have something to give him who has need. **Let** no corrupt word proceed out of your mouth, but what is good for necessary edification, that it may impart grace to the hearers. And do not grieve the Holy Spirit of God, by whom you were sealed for the day of redemption. **Let** all bitterness, wrath, anger, clamor, and evil speaking be put away from you, with all malice. And be kind to one another, tenderhearted, forgiving one another, even as God in Christ forgave you. -Ephesians 4:23-32

Nevertheless **let** each one of you in particular so love his own wife as himself, and **let** the wife *see* that she respects *her* husband. -Ephesians 5:33

Only **let** your conduct be worthy of the gospel of Christ, so that whether I come and see you or am absent, I may hear of your affairs, that you stand fast in one spirit, with one mind striving together for the faith of the gospel, -Philippians 1:27

Let nothing *be done* through selfish ambition or conceit, but in lowliness of mind **let** each esteem others better than himself. **Let** each of you look out not only for his own interests, but also for the interests of others. **Let** this mind be in you which was also in Christ Jesus, -Philippians 2:3-5

Let your gentleness be known to all men. The Lord *is* at hand. Be anxious for nothing, but in everything by prayer and supplication, with thanksgiving, **let** your requests be made known to God; and the peace of God, which surpasses all understanding, will guard your hearts and minds through Christ Jesus. -Philippians 4:5-6

And **let** the peace of God rule in your hearts, to which also you were called in one body; and be thankful. **Let** the word of Christ dwell in you richly in all wisdom, teaching and admonishing one another in psalms and hymns and spiritual songs, singing with grace in your hearts to the Lord. And whatever you *do* in word or deed, do all in the name of the Lord Jesus, giving thanks to God the Father through Him. -Colossians 3:15-17

Let them do good, that they be rich in good works, ready to give, willing to share, -1 Timothy 6:18

Nevertheless the solid foundation of God stands, having this seal: "The Lord knows those who are His," and, "**Let** everyone who names the name of Christ depart from iniquity." -2 Timothy 2:19

Speak these things, exhort, and rebuke with all authority. **Let** no one despise you. -Titus 2:15

And **let** our *people* also learn to maintain good works, to *meet* urgent needs, that they may not be unfruitful. -Titus 3:14

Yes, brother, **let** me have joy from you in the Lord; refresh my heart in the Lord. -Philemon 1:20

Let us therefore be diligent to enter that rest, lest anyone fall according to the same example of disobedience. For the word of God *is* living and powerful, and sharper than any two-edged sword, piercing even to the division of soul and spirit, and of joints and marrow, and is a discerner of the thoughts and intents of the heart. And there is no creature hidden from His sight, but all things are naked and open to the eyes of Him to whom we *must give* account. Seeing then that we have a great High Priest who has passed through the heavens, Jesus the Son of God, **let** us hold fast *our* confession. For we do not have a High Priest who cannot sympathize with our weaknesses, but was in all *points* tempted *as we are*, yet without sin. **Let** us therefore come boldly to the throne of grace, that we may obtain mercy and find grace to help in time of need. -Hebrews 4:11-16

Therefore, brethren, having boldness to enter the Holiest by the blood of Jesus, by a new and living way which He consecrated for us, through the veil, that is, His flesh, and *having* a High Priest over the house of God, **let** us draw near with a true heart in full assurance of faith, having our hearts sprinkled from an evil conscience and our bodies washed with pure water. **Let** us hold fast the confession of *our* hope without wavering, for He who promised *is* faithful. And **let** us consider one another in order to stir up love and good works, not forsaking the assembling of ourselves together, as *is* the manner of some, but exhorting *one another*, and so much the more as you see the Day approaching. -Hebrews 10:19-25

Therefore we also, since we are surrounded by so great a cloud of witnesses, **let** us lay aside every weight, and the sin which so easily ensnares *us*, and **let** us run with endurance the race that is set before us, -Hebrews 12:1

Therefore, since we are receiving a kingdom which cannot be shaken, **let** us have grace, by which we may serve God acceptably with reverence and godly fear. -Hebrews 12:28

Let brotherly love continue. -Hebrews 13:1

Let your conduct be without covetousness; be content with such things as you have. For He Himself has said, "I will never leave you nor forsake you." -Hebrews 13:5

Obey those who rule over you, and be submissive, for they watch out for your souls, as those who must give account. **Let** them do so with joy and not with grief, for that would be unprofitable for you. -Hebrews 13:17

But **let** patience have *its* perfect work, that you may be perfect and complete, lacking nothing. If any of you lacks wisdom, **let** him ask of God, who gives to all liberally and without reproach, and it will be given to him. But **let** him ask in faith, with no doubting, for he who doubts is like a wave of the sea driven and tossed by the wind. For **let** not that man suppose that he will receive anything from the Lord; *he is* a double-minded man, unstable in all his ways. -James 1:4-8

Let no one say when he is tempted, "I am tempted by God"; for God cannot be tempted by evil, nor does He Himself tempt anyone. -James 1:13

So then, my beloved brethren, **let** every man be swift to hear, slow to speak, slow to wrath; -James 1:19

Who *is* wise and understanding among you? **Let** him show by good conduct *that* his works *are done* in the meekness of wisdom. -James 3:13

But above all, my brethren, do not swear, either by heaven or by earth or with any other oath. But **let** your "Yes" be "Yes," and your "No," "No," lest you fall into judgment. Is anyone among you suffering? **Let** him pray. Is anyone cheerful? **Let** him sing psalms. Is anyone among you sick? **Let** him call for the elders of the church, and **let** them pray over him, anointing him with oil in the name of the Lord. And the prayer of faith will save the sick, and the Lord will raise him up. And if he has committed sins, he will be forgiven. Confess *your* trespasses to one another, and pray for one another, that you may be healed. The effective, fervent prayer of a righteous man avails much. -James 5:12-16

[L]et him know that he who turns a sinner from the error of his way will save a soul from death and cover a multitude of sins. -James 5:20

Finally, all *of you be* of one mind, having compassion for one another; love as brothers, *be* tenderhearted, *be* courteous; not returning evil for evil or reviling for reviling, but on the contrary blessing, knowing that you were called to this, that you may inherit a blessing. For "He who would love life and see good days, **let** him refrain his tongue from evil, and his lips from speaking deceit. **Let** him turn away from evil and do good; **let** him seek peace and pursue it. For the eyes of the Lord *are* on the righteous, and His ears *are open* to their prayers; but the face of the Lord *is* against those who do evil." -1 Peter 3:8-12

If anyone speaks, *let him speak* as the oracles of God. If anyone ministers, *let him do it* as with the ability which God supplies, that in all things God may be glorified through Jesus Christ, to whom belong the glory and the dominion forever and ever. Amen. -1 Peter 4:11

Yet if *anyone suffers* as a Christian, **let** him not be ashamed, but **let** him glorify God in this matter. -1 Peter 4:16

Therefore **let** that abide in you which you heard from the beginning. If what you heard from the beginning abides in you, you also will abide in the Son and in the Father. -1 John 2:24

Little children, **let** no one deceive you. He who practices righteousness is righteous, just as He is righteous. -1 John 3:7

Beloved, **let** us love one another, for love is of God; and everyone who loves is born of God and knows God. -1 John 4:7

"He who has an ear, **let** him hear what the Spirit says to the churches. To him who overcomes I will give to eat from the tree of life, which is in the midst of the Paradise of God." ' -Revelation 2:7

Let us be glad and rejoice and give Him glory, for the marriage of the Lamb has come, and His wife has made herself ready." - Revelation 9:7

And the Spirit and the bride say, "Come!" And **let** him who hears say, "Come!" And **let** him who thirsts come. Whoever desires, **let** him take the water of life freely. -Revelation 22:17

1: Resistance

Every promise of God is met with resistance. Pastor Beckford teaches, "Every man's promised land is surrounded by giants."

Resistance is opposition in the form of pushes and pulls. When looking at the word *resistance*, two words come into view, *resist* and *stance*. Resist the pushes and pulls of life, working to move you from *your* victory stance. The Bible identifies this as the *warring* spirit.

> For I delight in the law of God according to the inward man. But I see another law in my members, warring against the law of my mind, and bringing me into captivity to the law of sin which is in my members.
>
> -Romans 7:22-23

Scripturally, sin is whatever is *not* done from faith. A missed mark is an abandoned target.

> But he who doubts is condemned if he eats, because *he does* not *eat* from faith; for whatever *is* not from faith is sin.
>
> -Romans 14:23

Resistance strives to push you away from the goal and pull you off course, so you no longer engage in pursuit. Circumspectly, this is not a physical force. The warfare takes place in the mind to deter you from hitting the target - what God has already prepared beforehand for you to walk in.

Sometimes resistance is obvious and other times we are oblivious to it because it is so subtle – distraction, delay, or discouragement. And usually, they fall in that order.

We become distracted by the cares of this world (our day-to-day routines, our financial situation, lack, unproductive relationships, etc.), the opinions of others, or what we want now in lieu of making an investment in our future.

Those common distractions bring delays. Delays lead to discouragement and the dysfunctional cycle continues around and around again.

Unavoidable tragedy and unexpected pitfalls can become deterrents, as well. Maneuvering through, recovering, and healing from the difficulties of life, takes time. The cunningness of the enemy then says, we missed our opportunity and are past the time of possibility. But God is a redeemer of time, and His word will never pass away, "Heaven and earth will pass away, but My words will by no means pass away" (Luke 21:33). Please continue to move forward in the promises of God. It is not too late.

> Commit your works to the Lord [submit and trust them to Him], and your plans will succeed [if you respond to His will and guidance]. The Lord has made everything for its own purpose, even the wicked [according to their role] for the day of evil.
>
> -Proverbs 16:3-4 AMP

The warring spirit of resistance is there to persuade and convince you to forfeit. The solution is to transform the mind by evicting opposing thoughts and planting the victorious language of God, which is faith.

And do not be conformed to this world, but be transformed by the renewing of your mind, that you may prove what *is* that good and acceptable and perfect will of God.

-Romans 12:2

For the weapons of our warfare *are* not carnal but mighty in God for pulling down strongholds, casting down arguments and every high thing that exalts itself against the knowledge of God, bringing every thought into captivity to the obedience of Christ, and being ready to punish all disobedience when your obedience is fulfilled. Do you look at things according to the outward appearance? If anyone is convinced in himself that he is Christ's, let him again consider this in himself, that just as he *is* Christ's, even so we *are* Christ's.

-2 Corinthians 10:4-7

But what does it say? *"The word is near you, in your mouth and in your heart"* (that is, the word of faith which we preach):

-Romans 10:8

If anyone speaks, *let him speak* as the oracles of God. If anyone ministers, *let him do it* as with the ability which God supplies, that in all things God may be glorified through Jesus Christ, to whom belong the glory and the dominion forever and ever. Amen.

-1 Peter 4:11

. . .Indeed, let God be true but every man a liar. . .

-Romans 3:4

The power to overcome resistance manifests through the acknowledgement of the Holy Spirit and reliance on Him. We must be fully convinced and *Let it Happen!* God's word must be the final authority, in spite of what it may look like, sound like, or feel like to the senses.

He did not waver at the promise of God through unbelief, but was strengthened in faith, giving glory to God, and being fully convinced that what He had promised He was also able to perform. And therefore *"it was accounted to him for righteousness."*

-Romans 4:20-22

Jesus has gone "to prepare a place" for us in heaven and "will come again and receive" us to Himself, that where He is, we may be also (*see* John 14:2-3). While we are here to establish His kingdom on earth, "Your kingdom come. Your will be done on earth as *it is* in heaven" (Matthew 6:10). He has given us the gift of the Holy Spirit to help us overcome resistance and perpetually move forward, as well as reveal deception. His work is before Him, and His reward is with Him (*see* Isaiah 40:10 and Isaiah 62:11).

"These things I have spoken to you while being present with you. But the Helper, the Holy Spirit, whom the Father will send in My name, He will teach you all things, and bring to your remembrance all things that I said to you. Peace I leave with you, My peace I give to you; not as the world gives do I give to you. Let not your heart be troubled, neither let it be afraid. You have heard Me say to you, 'I am going away and coming *back* to you.' If you loved Me, you would rejoice because I said, 'I am going to the Father,' for My Father is greater than I. "And now I have told you before it comes, that when it does come to pass, you may believe. I will no longer talk much with you, for the ruler of this world is coming, and he has nothing in Me. But that the world may know that I love the Father, and as the Father gave Me commandment, so I do. Arise, let us go from here.

-John 14:25-31

Beloved, do not believe every spirit, but test the spirits, whether they are of God; because many false prophets have gone out into the world. By this you know the Spirit of God: Every spirit that confesses that Jesus Christ has come in the flesh is of God, and every spirit that does not confess that Jesus Christ has come in the flesh is not of God. And this is the *spirit* of the Antichrist, which you have heard was coming, and is now already in the world. You are of God, little children, and have overcome them, because He who is in you is greater than he who is in the world. They are of the world. Therefore they speak *as* of the world, and the world hears them. We are of God. He who knows God hears us; he who is not of God does not hear us. By this we know the spirit of truth and the spirit of error. Beloved, let us love one another, for love is of God; and everyone who loves is born of God and knows God. He who does not love does not know God, for God is love.

-1 John 4:1-8

Behold, the Lord God shall come with a strong *hand*, And His arm shall rule for Him; Behold, His reward *is* with Him, And His work before Him.

-Isaiah 40:10

Indeed the Lord has proclaimed to the end of the world: "Say to the daughter of Zion, 'Surely your salvation is coming; behold, His reward *is* with Him, and His work before Him.' "

-Isaiah 62:11

We are already blessed by God. We don't have to earn the blessing or pay for the blessing. We have been blessed from the beginning (*see* Genesis 1:22, Genesis 1:28, and Genesis 5:2).

We are already gifted by God. The gift is within us and must be *stirred* up through action and even agitation. The spirit of fear is to resist you from operating in your gift. God has given us power, love, and a sound mind to navigate resistance. Remember, the place where your foot fits (the precepts) is the place where you will profit. "And you shall remember the Lord your God, for *it is* He who gives you power to get wealth, that He may establish His covenant which He swore to your fathers, as *it is* this day" (Deuteronomy 8:18).

When we do all things as to the Lord, He causes them to prosper. A wisdom is available by the Spirit of God to produce wonders in the earth through us, His beloved.

However, we speak wisdom among those who are mature, yet not the wisdom of this age, nor of the rulers of this age, who are coming to nothing. But we speak the wisdom of God in a mystery, the hidden *wisdom* which God ordained before the ages for our glory, which none of the rulers of this age knew; for had they known, they would not have crucified the Lord of glory. But as it is written: *"Eye has not seen, nor ear heard, nor have entered into the heart of man the things which God has prepared for those who love Him."* But God has revealed *them* to us through His Spirit. For the Spirit searches all things, yes, the deep things of God. For what man knows the things of a man except the spirit of the man which is in him? Even so no one knows the things of God except the Spirit of God. Now we have received, not the spirit of the world, but the Spirit who is from God, that we might know the things that have been freely given to us by God. These things we also speak, not in words which man's wisdom teaches but which the Holy Spirit teaches, comparing spiritual things with spiritual. But the natural man does not receive the things of the Spirit of God, for they are foolishness to him; nor can he know *them*, because they are spiritually discerned. But he who is spiritual judges all things, yet he himself is *rightly* judged by no one. For *"who has known the mind of the Lord that he may instruct Him?"* But we have the mind of Christ.

-1 Corinthians 2:6-16

Believe you are already blessed.

Blessed *be* the God and Father of our Lord Jesus Christ, who has blessed us with every spiritual blessing in the heavenly *places* in Christ,
-Ephesians 1:3

Know you are already gifted.

Therefore I remind you to stir up the gift of God which is in you through the laying on of my hands. For God has not given us a spirit of fear, but of power and of love and of a sound mind.
-2 Timothy 1:6-7

Do all things as unto the Lord.

And whatever you do, do it heartily, as to the Lord and not to men, knowing that from the Lord you will receive the reward of the inheritance; for you serve the Lord Christ.
-Colossians 3:23-24

2: Recompense

Let God arise,
Let His enemies be scattered;
Let those also who hate Him flee before Him.

-Psalm 68:1

Recompense is the gift of God's defense with restitution. In the earthly court system, restitution is not just a dollar-for-dollar reimbursement. The total due is calculated to include other factors, such as physical and emotional pain and suffering, loss of use or income or even potential income, etc.

Do not say, "I will recompense evil";
Wait for the Lord, and He will save you.

-Proverbs 20:22

This is why the Bible admonishes us to overcome evil with good.

Repay no one evil for evil. Have regard for good things in the sight of all men. If it is possible, as much as depends on you, live peaceably with all men. Beloved, do not avenge yourselves, but *rather* give place to wrath; for it is written, *"Vengeance is Mine, I will repay,"* says the Lord. Therefore *"If your enemy is hungry, feed him; If he is thirsty, give him a drink; For in so doing you will heap coals of fire on his head."* Do not be overcome by evil, but overcome evil with good.

-Romans 12:17-21

But let patience have *its* perfect work, that you may be perfect and complete, lacking nothing. If any of you lacks wisdom, let him ask of God, who gives to all liberally and without reproach, and it will be given to him.

-James 1:4-5

And you will be hated by all for My name's sake. But not a hair of your head shall be lost. By your patience possess your souls.

-Luke 21:18-19

One God-given assignment for this book, *Let it Happen*, is to remind believers to focus on establishing the kingdom of God by directly operating in His principles. Recompense must be enforced spiritually, but not plotted naturally.

At times, we may be the one on the side of error, known or unknown, and it is always better to be convicted by the Holy Spirit than condemned by man. Conviction repairs, condemnation destroys.

Fear not, for I *am* with you; be not dismayed, for I *am* your God. I will strengthen you, yes, I will help you, I will uphold you with My righteous right hand.' "Behold, all those who were incensed against you shall be ashamed and disgraced; they shall be as nothing, and those who strive with you shall perish. You shall seek them and not find them—those who contended with you. Those who war against you shall be as nothing, as a nonexistent thing. For I, the Lord your God, will hold your right hand, saying to you, 'Fear not, I will help you.'

-Isaiah 41:10-13

Put Me in remembrance; let us contend together; State your *case*, that you may be acquitted.

-Isaiah 43:26

But if you indeed obey His voice and do all that I speak, then I will be an enemy to your enemies and an adversary to your adversaries.

-Exodus 23:22

Give God the space to deal with those who have hurt you. The grace you extend, even to a person who intentionally, deliberately, and spitefully sinned against you, may be the *saving* grace they meditate on when they are in despair.

The prodigal son was alone in the midst of his mess, when he came to himself and said, "How many of my father's hired servants have bread enough and to spare, and I perish with hunger!" (*see* Luke 15:17). The prodigal son was in error. He sinned against his father and made a series of decisions that led to his downfall. But he had the example of his father's grace to meditate on that strengthened him and led him to restoration.

While our emotions may want God to slay our enemies immediately, the greatest victory and glory to God comes through conviction producing a changed heart, and a changed life.

Therefore I say to you, her sins, *which are* many, are forgiven, for she loved much. But to whom little is forgiven, *the same* loves little."

-Luke 7:47

The above verse comes from Jesus' response to spectators who did not understand the principle of recompense.

A woman seeking a fresh start brought an alabaster flask of expensive fragrant oil to anoint Jesus' feet. She was judged for her future when her investment was called a waste. She was judged for her past when the Pharisee spoke to himself, degrading the woman – "who and what manner of woman *this is* touching Him, for she is a sinner" (*see* Luke 7:39).

But while man was going down her sin record to belittle her and count her out, Jesus was going down her mercy record which clearly calculated the greatness of her value.

Meditate on His mercy which has been poured out over your life. We have been spared from our own habitual intentional sin because God has *all-ready* made an investment in us with confidence that His words and intentions for us are the final authority. My dad's go-to response to the questioning of my siblings and myself was always, "Because I said so!"

We are to be ready to punish all disobedience when our obedience is fulfilled (*see* 2 Corinthians 10:6). You are an asset to the kingdom of God. Let grace do its perfect work.

But may the God of all grace, who called us to His eternal glory by Christ Jesus, after you have suffered a while, perfect, establish, strengthen, and settle *you*.

-1 Peter 5:10

Joseph said to them, "Do not be afraid, for *am* I in the place of God? But as for you, you meant evil against me; *but* God meant it for good, in order to bring it about as *it is* this day, to save many people alive. Now therefore, do not be afraid; I will provide for you and your little ones." And he comforted them and spoke kindly to them.

-Genesis 50:19-21

There are many systems of the world that are crooked and not operating in alignment within the principles and intentions of God. "When the righteous are in authority, the people rejoice; but when a wicked *man* rules, the people groan" (Proverbs 29:2).

This is why it is imperative that the solution to the world's problems within you be activated. The people who will benefit from it and the people who are assigned to utilize their gifts in collaboration to bring it forth are waiting, "For the earnest expectation of the creation eagerly waits for the revealing of the sons of God" (Romans 8:19).

God wants us to move forward to take possession of greater and mightier, than we can strive to obtain in our own strength.

"Hear, O Israel: You are to cross over the Jordan today, and go in to dispossess nations greater and mightier than yourself, cities great and fortified up to heaven, a people great and tall, the descendants of the Anakim, whom you know, and *of whom* you heard *it said*, 'Who can stand before the descendants of Anak?' 3 Therefore understand today that the Lord your God is He who goes over before you as a consuming fire. He will destroy them and bring them down before you; so you shall drive them out and destroy them quickly, as the Lord has said to you. "Do not think in your heart, after the Lord your God has cast them out before you, saying, 'Because of my righteousness the Lord has brought me in to possess this land'; but it is because of the wickedness of these nations *that* the Lord is driving them out from before you. *It is* not because of your righteousness or the uprightness of your heart *that* you go in to possess their land, but because of the wickedness of these nations *that* the Lord your God drives them out from before you, and that He may fulfill the word which the Lord swore to your fathers, to Abraham, Isaac, and Jacob.

-Deuteronomy 9:1-5

We condemn ourselves because of past behavior or imperfections the enemy magnifies to cause us to feel like we don't deserve it or can't do it. God is seeking those who will not waiver in their tenacity and stand for what is right. God through Jesus Christ established our righteousness, to make us usable. Therefore, the questions become:

- ✓ Is the endeavor just and serve the people of God?
- ✓ Do we have faith in God to do His part?
- ✓ And are we willing and obedient to do our part?

[Y]et because this widow troubles me I will avenge her, lest by her continual coming she weary me.' " Then the Lord said, "Hear what the unjust judge said. And shall God not avenge His own elect who cry out day and night to Him, though He bears long with them? I tell you that He will avenge them speedily. Nevertheless, when the Son of Man comes, will He really find faith on the earth?"

-Luke 18:5-8

No weapon formed against you shall prosper, and every tongue *which* rises against you in judgment You shall condemn. This *is* the heritage of the servants of the Lord, and their righteousness *is* from Me," Says the Lord.

-Isaiah 54:17

So Jesus answered and said to them, "Have faith in God.["]

-Mark 11:22

Therefore, having been justified by faith, we have peace with God through our Lord Jesus Christ, through whom also we have access by faith into this grace in which we stand, and rejoice in hope of the glory of God.

-Romans 5:1-2

If you are willing and obedient, you shall eat the good of the land;

-Isaiah 1:19

God is ready to move the wicked and unjust out of position. Concurrently, the people of God must be willing to move forward.

What if every ungodly political, business, educational, industry, and community leader were evicted from their role today? Are there enough prepared Christians to move into those positions?

The Lord released the promised land little by little, at the rate of His people's preparedness, willingness, and forward progress.

Little by little I will drive them out from before you, until you have increased, and you inherit the land.

-Exodus 23:30

And the Lord your God will drive out those nations before you little by little; you will be unable to destroy them at once, lest the beasts of the field become too numerous for you.

-Deuteronomy 7:22

3: Reconciliation

To reconcile is to balance. When a financial account is reconciled, the credits and debits are accounted for and confirmed. When a relationship is reconciled, the people involved come to an agreement to move forward from the past into the future. Reconciliation is not a denial of the things that 'took away' from the finances or the relationship. It is a quality decision to 'add to' what is left.

To *Let it Happen*, we must balance resistance and recompense. Resistance is the enemy's attempt to stop it and recompense is God's great desire and influence for full manifestation despite every contrary circumstance and adversary.

Often because we know God *can* do it, we expect God to do it without any action on our part. Our part is to be a doer of the possible and let God do the impossible and for us to do the controllable and let God do the uncontrollable. God works in partnership with us and equips us with grace to do our part.

> But he who looks into the perfect law of liberty and continues *in it*, and is not a forgetful hearer but a doer of the work, this one will be blessed in what he does.
>
> -James 1:25

> We then, *as* workers together *with Him* also plead with *you* not to receive the grace of God in vain.
>
> -2 Corinthians 6:1

God does not expect us to do anything with things we do not have. However, He does expect us to do every-thing we can with what we have. We cannot Biblically justify inaction and stagnation.

> And in this I give advice: It is to your advantage not only to be doing what you began and were desiring to do a year ago; but now you also must complete the doing *of it*; that as *there was* a readiness to desire *it*, so *there* also *may be* a completion out of what *you* have. For if there is first a willing mind, *it is* accepted according to what one has, *and* not according to what he does not have.
>
> -2 Corinthians 8:10-12

When the widow in 2 Kings 4 cried out to Elisha, in fear of her sons being taken as slaves by the creditor, he asked her, "Tell me, what do you have in the house?" (see 2 Kings 4:2). Before Elisha prompted her to consider what she *already* had, she was distraught and hopeless. When she discovered what she *all-ready* had and followed the strategic directions of the man of God, she was able to generate income to pay her debt and live on the profit.

In Exodus 3, Moses was tending the flock of his father-in-law with a rod in his hand when he turned aside to communicate with God. They had an honest conver-sation. The Lord gave Moses instruction, "Come now, therefore, and I will send you to Pharaoh that you may bring My people, the children of Israel, out of Egypt" (Exodus 3:10).

Moses was indecisive and lacked confidence. "So the Lord said to him, 'What is that in your hand?' Moses responded, "A rod" (*see* Exodus 4:2). The Lord and Moses immediately entered into a one-on-one time of preparation and training.

> And He said, "Cast it on the ground." So he cast it on the ground, and it became a serpent; and Moses fled from it. Then the Lord said to Moses, "Reach out your hand and take *it* by the tail" (and he reached out his hand and caught it, and it became a rod in his hand), "that they may believe that the Lord God of their fathers, the God of Abraham, the God of Isaac, and the God of Jacob, has appeared to you." Furthermore the Lord said to him, "Now put your hand in your bosom." And he put his hand in his bosom, and when he took it out, behold, his hand *was* leprous, like snow. And He said, "Put your hand in your bosom again." So he put his hand in his bosom again, and drew it out of his bosom, and behold, it was restored like his *other* flesh.
>
> -Exodus 4:3-7

Moses *all-ready* had the rod in his hand. The rod was his training instrument to overcome fear. In Egypt, Aaron threw down his rod and it became a serpent. The wise men, sorcerers, and magicians also threw down their rods and they became serpents. Ultimately, Aaron's rod swallowed up the other rods (*see* Exodus 7:9-12). Moses was sent to Egypt by God to deliver God's people and to be made *as* God to Pharaoh (*see* Exodus 7:1). If Moses did not overcome his fear of serpents and practice operating in power during his alone time with God, he would have crumpled in fear.

When the Lord directed Moses to put his hand in his bosom for the first time, it became leprous. The second time it was restored. The first time Moses was in Egypt it ended in destruction. God was sending him back to the place of his greatest defeat to deliver His very own beloved people. Moses had to be assured that reconciliation was possible, and God's power would show up, in the same place that once broke him down. Forty years prior, Moses fled Egypt as a fugitive. Now, he was sent back to be a leader and a liberator.

The ten plagues took place as a demonstration of God's ultimate power. The first three plagues came to pass by the hand of Aaron, as directed by Moses, who was given the commands by God.

The next two plagues were performed by the Lord after Moses announced them to Pharoah, under the instruction of the Lord.

Moses' hand wasn't set in action until the sixth, seventh, eighth, and ninth plagues. The tenth plague was performed by God.

When they left Egypt, they followed the 'road map' God provided. The route landed them on a peninsula confronted with the impossibility of the Red Sea before them and the Egyptian army behind them, desiring their return to hard bondage.

Have you ever followed God's directions and ended up at a place of impossibility, wondering where you went wrong, and where is God? Well, God was there, and He was ready to perform His word. It was time for Moses to use the rod, that once terrified him, to gain victory for the Lord, himself, and over six hundred thousand people who crossed over with him (*see* Exodus 12:37).

> And Moses said to the people, "Do not be afraid. Stand still, and see the salvation of the Lord, which He will accomplish for you today. For the Egyptians whom you see today, you shall see again no more forever. The Lord will fight for you, and you shall hold your peace." And the Lord said to Moses, "Why do you cry to Me? Tell the children of Israel to go forward. But lift up your rod, and stretch out your hand over the sea and divide it. And the children of Israel shall go on dry *ground* through the midst of the sea.

-Exodus 14:13-16

Moses' story emphasizes, to *Let it Happen*, we must believe three key facts to bring to completion each thing that is written about us in the book of heaven:

- ✓ God wants to do it
- ✓ He wants to do it through us
- ✓ *And* we are equipped to carry out the assignment

Moses grew with God and in God, to do God's will. When we look at Scriptures demonstrating God's power working through people, without reviewing the process of preparation before the performance of the word, we feel inadequate and unqualified, just like Moses did initially. We must reconcile within ourselves; it is His power working within us to do exceedingly and abundantly more than we could ever do on our own.

Now to Him who is able to [carry out His purpose and] do superabundantly more than all that we dare ask or think [infinitely beyond our greatest prayers, hopes, or dreams], according to His power that is at work within us,

-Ephesians 3:20 AMP

Paul, previously called Saul, in the New Testament, had to forsake the misconceptions and guilt from his former lifestyle and receive reconciliation through Jesus Christ.

Saul was trained by the elite of the world to believe and religiously practice misconceptions. He shares his testimony as often as he can in the thirteen epistles he wrote to instruct, correct, strengthen, and encourage people who lived in his time, and those of us who came after, still reading his words preserved in the Bible. He lays out his religious qualifications, then boldly declares it was all nothing without reconciliation, partnership, and life in Christ.

[T]hough I also might have confidence in the flesh. If anyone else thinks he may have confidence in the flesh, I more so: circumcised the eighth day, of the stock of Israel, of the tribe of Benjamin, a Hebrew of the Hebrews; concerning the law, a Pharisee; concerning zeal, persecuting the church; concerning the righteousness which is in the law, blameless. But what things were gain to me, these I have counted loss for Christ. Yet indeed I also count all things loss for the excellence of the knowledge of Christ Jesus my Lord, for whom I have suffered the loss of all things, and count them as rubbish, that I may gain Christ and be found in Him, not having my own righteousness, which *is* from the law, but that which *is* through faith in Christ, the righteousness which is from God by faith; that I may know Him and the power of His resurrection, and the fellowship of His sufferings, being conformed to His death, if, by any means, I may attain to the resurrection from the dead. Not that I have already attained, or am already perfected; but I press on, that I may lay hold of that for which Christ Jesus has also laid hold of me. Brethren, I do not count myself to have apprehended; but one thing *I do*, forgetting those things which are behind and reaching forward to those things which are ahead, I press toward the goal for the prize of the upward call of God in Christ Jesus. Therefore let us, as many as are mature, have this mind; and if in anything you think otherwise, God will reveal even this to you. Nevertheless, to *the degree* that we have already attained, let us walk by the same rule, let us be of the same mind.

-Philippians 3:4-16

"I am indeed a Jew, born in Tarsus of Cilicia, but brought up in this city at the feet of Gamaliel, taught according to the strictness of our fathers' law, and was zealous toward God as you all are today. I persecuted this Way to the death, binding and delivering into prisons both men and women, as also the high priest bears me witness, and all the council of the elders, from whom I also received letters to the brethren, and went to

Damascus to bring in chains even those who were there to Jerusalem to be punished.["]

-Acts 22: 3-5

And I thank Christ Jesus our Lord who has enabled me, because He counted me faithful, putting *me* into the ministry, although I was formerly a blasphemer, a persecutor, and an insolent man; but I obtained mercy because I did *it* ignorantly in unbelief. And the grace of our Lord was exceedingly abundant, with faith and love which are in Christ Jesus. This *is* a faithful saying and worthy of all acceptance, that Christ Jesus came into the world to save sinners, of whom I am chief. However, for this reason I obtained mercy, that in me first Jesus Christ might show all longsuffering, as a pattern to those who are going to believe on Him for everlasting life. Now to the King eternal, immortal, invisible, to God who alone is wise, *be* honor and glory forever and ever. Amen.

-1 Timothy 1:12-17

While Saul was actively resisting and attempting to destroy the impact of Christ, the Lord called him, "a chosen vessel of Mine" to preach the gospel before "Gentiles, kings, and the children of Israel" (*see* Acts 9:15).

God's plan prevailed even the infiltration of religion, and the undeniable shame connected to the things Saul did in his past.

His monumental teachings elaborate on mercy, grace, mind transformation, perseverance, order, triumphing through trials and tribulations, relationships among people, and the ultimate authority and headship of Jesus Christ.

He reconciled; he exchanged his mind for the mind of Christ. The mind of Christ is available to us all. We must *Let it Happen*, by forsaking the former natural and carnal mind - which is our old way of thinking, reasoning, and drawing conclusions without considering the principles of God.

> For those who live according to the flesh set their minds on the things of the flesh, but those *who live* according to the Spirit, the things of the Spirit. For to be carnally minded is death, but to be spiritually minded is life and peace. Because the carnal mind *is* enmity against God; for it is not subject to the law of God, nor indeed can be.
>
> -Romans 8:5-7

Let this mind be in you which was also in Christ Jesus,

-Philippians 2:5

[H]ow much more shall the blood of Christ, who through the eternal Spirit offered Himself without spot to God, cleanse your conscience from dead works to serve the living God?

-Hebrews 9:14

The same blood of Christ we believe was shed for the forgiveness of our sins was also shed for the cleansing of our conscience from dead works so we can confidently serve the living God. That means we do not have to continually replay the shame and devastation of sin and trauma. The factual memory still exists but the emotional torment and pain subsides, and we find it to be true, "My grace is sufficient for you, for My strength is made perfect in weakness" (*see* 2 Corinthians 12:9).

4: Response

Reactions are not responses. Reactions are usually spontaneous based on instinct or emotion.

Responses take into consideration various factors, count the associated costs (financial, emotional, relational, time, etc.), and weigh the possible outcomes.

The word of God and His directives require a response. Mary responded, "Behold the maidservant of the Lord! Let it be to me according to your word," when the angel presented her with the work of the Holy Spirit, she was created to conceive, carry, and care for (*see* Luke 1:30-38).

In Mary's response, she identified herself as a maidservant of the Lord. We are also made-to-serve the Lord. Because she knew it was God who said it, she willingly submitted to it. She asked the question in Luke 1:34, "How can this be, since I do not know a man?" and it is confirmed in Matthew 1:25 that there was no human influence or interference credited to Jesus' entrance into the earth, "and [Joseph] did not know her till she had brought forth her firstborn Son. And he called His name Jesus."

Mary and Joseph both had to forsake their own plans and intentionally align their lives more closely with God to fulfill their assignment. It required more strategic guidance from God and less conversation with people. Joseph had an ability to see and Mary willingly submitted to Joseph's headship and role as the protector.

Joseph had his own encounter, to confirm that the Child was conceived of the Holy Spirit. Because he knew this was of God, he was not moved by the resistance of opinion and custom. When we have the assurance that something is of God, we don't ask people their opinion. Knowing *this* is happening is the foundation. Then we must keep our eyes out for the provision for the vision as we embark on the route.

Joseph was in tune and responsive to each of the four recorded encounters he had with the angel of the Lord, as he was guided to lead his family and protect Jesus Christ (*see* Matthew 1:20, Matthew 2:13, Matthew 2:19, Matthew 2:22).

We must be able to still see when adversity comes to blindfold us. When we have already seen what God has said in our inner man, by the Spirit, we can maneuver and go forward.

> For a great and effective door has opened to me, and there are many adversaries.

> -1 Corinthians 16:9

> Now when He was asked by the Pharisees when the kingdom of God would come, He answered them and said, "The kingdom of God does not come with observation; nor will they say, 'See here!' or 'See there!' For indeed, the kingdom of God is within you."

> -Luke 17:20-21

Jesus clearly told us that the kingdom of God is within us, and it does not come by observation. We must be doers of the word, and the word awakens the desire to do the God-given work assigned to us (*see* James 1:22-25). We are not saved by works. However, we are saved to serve. Our salvation is a gift of God (*see* Ephesians 2:8-9) and the realization of our purpose becomes our priority.

1 Samuel 1 demonstrates Hannah's transition from reacting to responding. She was a barren woman, unable to produce a child, and provoked by the prosperity of another woman. She acknowledged that her prayers, up until the time of her realization, were "out of the abundance of my complaint and grief" (*see* 1 Samuel 1:9-16).

Year by year, her prayers originated from a sorrowful spirit, bitterness of the soul, and anguish; a reaction of complaints and grief. This day, in truth, she responded by purging in the place of prayer. She surrendered her situation to God. Her response was in the form of a vow.

> Then she made a vow and said, "O Lord of hosts, if You will indeed look on the affliction of Your maidservant and remember me, and not forget Your maidservant, but will give Your maid-servant a male child, then I will give him to the Lord all the days of his life, and no razor shall come upon his head."
>
> -1 Samuel 1:11

Once Hannah rid herself from the sabotage of her emotional reactions, and responded in accordance to Godly purpose, her petition became her reality over time.

Then Eli answered and said, "Go in peace, and the God of Israel grant your petition which you have asked of Him." And she said, "Let your maidservant find favor in your sight." So the woman went her way and ate, and her face was no longer sad.

-1 Samuel 1:17-18

In 1 Samuel 2, Hannah's prayer language changed from pity to prosperity as she incorporated the strength of the word of God into her prayers.

He will guard the feet of His saints, but the wicked shall be silent in darkness. "For by strength no man shall prevail. The adversaries of the Lord shall be broken in pieces; from heaven He will thunder against them. The Lord will judge the ends of the earth. "He will give strength to His king, and exalt the horn of His anointed."

-1 Samuel 2:9-10

In critical situations, when people are ready to come to the end of themselves, even people who don't closely recognize God in their lives, they make bold promises to God. Fill in the blank, "God if You _____, I will never _____." Or "God if You _____, I will always _____." This tells me, that most people know what behavior causes their downfalls, and what behavior will elevate their lives.

For then you will have your delight in the Almighty, and lift up your face to God. You will make your prayer to Him, He will hear you, and you will pay your vows. You will also declare a thing, and it will be established for you; so light will shine on your ways.

-Job 22:26-28

The establishment of a thing is at its declaration. Light then shines on *our* ways so we know how to do it, and we *must* do it.

God does not withhold any good thing from us. He is a good Father. Often, we don't have because we have not asked the One who beholds the blueprint and is able to produce it. Or we have received but not yet yielded ourselves to the developmental process.

When we look to man, we are disappointed. When we look to God, we are appointed. Answers to our prayers require wisdom to cultivate them to their highest potential. Wisdom, grace, and the power of the Holy Spirit are heavenly packaged with every great exploit.

For the Lord God is a sun and shield; the Lord will give grace and glory; no good *thing* will He withhold from those who walk uprightly.

-Psalm 84:11

"So I say to you, ask, and it will be given to you; seek, and you will find; knock, and it will be opened to you. For everyone who asks receives, and he who seeks finds, and to him who knocks it will be opened. If a son asks for bread from any father among you, will he give him a stone? Or if *he* asks for a fish, will he give him a serpent instead of a fish? Or if he asks for an egg, will he offer him a scorpion? If you then, being evil, know how to give good gifts to your children, how much more will *your* heavenly Father give the Holy Spirit to those who ask Him!"

-Luke 11:9-13

Until now you have asked nothing in My name. Ask, and you will receive, that your joy may be full.

-John 16:24

But the wisdom that is from above is first pure, then peaceable, gentle, willing to yield, full of mercy and good fruits, without partiality and without hypocrisy. Now the fruit of righteousness is sown in peace by those who make peace.

-James 3:17-18

Peace is the key indicator of the direction to go when responding to the requests of others or solidifying the call of God on your life. Peace is a prepared place. Peace is to be pursued. Peace is surety that your feet are landing in the precepts predetermined before your conception. Peace is possible even in the midst of contrary circumstances and captivity.

Depart from evil and do good; seek peace and pursue it.

-Psalm 34:14

Therefore let us pursue the things *which make* for peace and the things by which one may edify another.

-Romans 14:19

Flee also youthful lusts; but pursue righteousness, faith, love, peace with those who call on the Lord out of a pure heart.

-2 Timothy 2:22

Pursue peace with all *people*, and holiness, without which no one will see the Lord:

-Hebrews 12:14

Let him turn away from evil and do good; let him seek peace and pursue it.

-1 Peter 3:11

And the God of peace will crush Satan under your feet shortly. The grace of our Lord Jesus Christ be with you. Amen.

-Romans 16:20

When we are in the peace of God, Satan is crushed under our feet. Satan no longer has any temptation, distraction, or alternate route that appeals to us, because *we know that we know* we are walking in what God has established beforehand.

Therefore submit to God. Resist the devil and he will flee from you.

-James 4:7

Submitting to God is resisting the urge to come out from the place of obedience. The devil will present an option that partially meets our expectations and alleviates having to believe for the entire substance of things hoped for. When we make a quality decision to stand, the enemy will flee. Please know God is able to do exceedingly, abundantly above all that we ask or think, according to the power that works in us (*see* Ephesians 3:20). Don't settle for the part only. The *part* is infallible evidence there is a whole.

An often quoted Scripture is Jeremiah 29:11, "For I know the thoughts that I think toward you, says the Lord, thoughts of peace and not of evil, to give you a future and a hope." This enduring promise was declared to God's people when they were in a seventy year captivity. Notice, their captivity had an expiration date, and while they were in *that* situation, God assured them of His thoughts toward them. He also encouraged them to be at ease, partake in their prosperity, and increase generationally. Practically, we know children, grand-children, and great grandchildren require additional provision, and God was adamant that He would be faithful to all. He even assured the peace of the city, and their peace, as they prayed to the Lord.

> Build houses and dwell *in them*; plant gardens and eat their fruit. Take wives and beget sons and daughters; and take wives for your sons and give your daughters to husbands, so that they may bear sons and daughters—that you may be increased there, and not diminished. And seek the peace of the city where I have caused you to be carried away captive, and pray to the Lord for it; for in its peace you will have peace.
>
> -Jeremiah 29:5-7

We must acknowledge and glorify God who holds our breath in His hand and owns all our ways (*see* Daniel

5:23). The Bible tells us, "Pride *goes* before destruction, and a haughty spirit before a fall" (Proverbs 16:18). Let us *not* forsake His ways and His guidance. To prove the word, we must *do* the word (*see* Romans 12:2). Many people are noted in the Bible to have almost missed their opportunity for breakthrough because they reacted to the word instead of responding.

Naaman was a "commander of the army of the king of Syria, a great and honorable man in the eyes of his master, because by him the Lord had given victory to Syria. He was also a mighty man of valor, *but* a leper" (*see* 2 Kings 5:1). The king he served, sent a letter to the king of Israel saying, "Now be advised, when this letter comes to you, that I have sent Naaman my servant to you, that you may heal him of his leprosy" (*see* 2 Kings 5:6). The king of Israel quickly recognized it was *not* in his power to heal.

The servant girl originally said, "If only my master were with the prophet who *is* in Samaria! For he would heal him of his leprosy" (*see* 2 Kings 5:3). She did not credit the king of Israel as able to perform a healing miracle, but the king of Syria's mindset was *not* receptive to a prophet having power, so the petition was sent to the king.

So it was, when Elisha the man of God heard that the king of Israel had torn his clothes, that he sent to the king, saying, "Why have you torn your clothes? Please let him come to me, and he shall know that there is a prophet in Israel." Then Naaman went with his horses and chariot, and he stood at the door of Elisha's house. And Elisha sent a messenger to him, saying, "Go and wash in the Jordan seven times, and your flesh shall be restored to you, and *you shall* be clean." But Naaman became furious, and went away and said, "Indeed, I said to myself, 'He will surely come out *to me*, and stand and call on the name of the Lord his God, and wave his hand over the place, and heal the leprosy.' *Are* not the Abanah and the Pharpar, the rivers of Damascus, better than all the waters of Israel? Could I not wash in them and be clean?" So he turned and went away in a rage. And his servants came near and spoke to him, and said, "My father, *if* the prophet had told you *to do* something great, would you not have done *it*? How much more then, when he says to you, 'Wash, and be clean'?" So he went down and dipped seven times in the Jordan, according to the saying of the man of God; and his flesh was restored like the flesh of a little child, and he was clean. And he returned to the man of God, he and all his aides, and came and stood before him; and he said, "Indeed, now I know that *there is* no God in all the earth, except in Israel; now therefore, please take a gift from your servant." But he said, "As the Lord lives, before whom I stand, I will receive nothing." And he urged him to take *it*, but he refused.

-2 Kings 5:9-16

Naaman's initial reaction was offense. He *thought* he deserved the ritual of his imagination in which he *should* be honored by the prophet and automatically healed by the waving of his hand over the place, instead of having to perform an active role in obedience. His reaction was rooted in pride, making him furious, and in an emotional rage, he almost missed his healing.

He learned God when he responded by following the directions given and proved "what *is* that good and acceptable and perfect will of God" (*see* Romans 12:2).

Again, responses take into consideration various factors, count the associated costs (financial, emotional, relational, time, etc.), and weigh the possible outcomes.

Naaman considered various factors. He mentioned his version of the plan and the different rivers he felt were better options, he counted the associated costs (he already made the trip believing healing was his destination, his servants reminded Naaman he would have done 'something great' to be healed and encouraged him to respond to the directions given), he weighed the possible outcomes. He had the choice of going home the same or *to do* something to bring forth the change he desired. Ultimately, Naaman's response was to disregard his plan and *Let it Happen* – by responding to God's plan, in obedience to the prophet.

In Mark 10:46-48, Blind Bartimaeus responded to Jesus' presence with a loud cry, "Jesus, Son of David, have mercy on me!" Many people around him reacted and warned him to be quiet – determined he was acting out of order, but Bartimaeus continued his cry all the more, with an assurance that Jesus was the solution to the situation he was sitting in, as a blind beggar on the side of the road.

So Jesus stood still and commanded him to be called. Then they called the blind man, saying to him, "Be of good cheer. Rise, He is calling you." And throwing aside his garment, he rose and came to Jesus. So Jesus answered and said to him, "What do you want Me to do for you?" The blind man said to Him, "Rabboni, that I may receive my sight." Then Jesus said to him, "Go your way; your faith has made you well." And immediately he received his sight and followed Jesus on the road.

-Mark 10:49-52

When called by Jesus, Bartimaeus discarded the banner of blind beggar he wore as a garment. While everyone around him reacted by protocol, Bartimaeus responded by removing the mark of what he no longer wanted to be *before* he received the desire of his heart. His faith made him well, he received his sight, and followed Jesus. We must discard the titles we don't want to carry into our future to make space for the new and change our cry from pity to principle.

Psalm 23:3 tells us, "He restores my soul; He leads me in the paths of righteousness for His name's sake." Our soul is the reactive part (emotions, fickle feelings, and carnal thought patterns). To walk in the paths of righteousness for His name's sake is to respond to His word, His will, and the precepts for your life. Know He wants to bring forth the full manifestation of the plan and purpose for your life, more than you want it.

When an earthly will is read following someone's death, it cannot be changed by the opinion of others. The will of the writer, is the final authority. Jesus's died. He paid the ransom and the debt of sin, so we can walk in the inheritance and promises of His will. *Let it Happen!*

5: Results

"All *this,*" *said David,* "the Lord made me understand in writing, by *His* hand upon me, all the works of these plans."

-1 Chronicles 28:19

This section of the book is for you to plan, pursue, & record your progress. God gave me the mission, purpose, and vision for Transformed Publishing in June 2020 early one morning when I was sitting in my backyard on a group prayer call.

I had a vague idea to start a publishing company after the things I experienced as a first-time author but had not yet formed a tangible plan or focused my expectations.

That morning, I opened a notepad app on my phone and typed the words mission, purpose, and vision. I immediately filled in the information as it was downloaded into my mind by the Holy Spirit. Later, I sketched a rough draft of the logo I envisioned. That was the start. As I continued to write out the plan and expectations for Transformed Publishing in the upcoming weeks, understanding came and the work began, *proclaiming transformation and truth.*

Please email: transformedpublishing @gmail.com to share your *Let it Happen* testimonies and to place bulk book orders:
25 books for $150
50 books for $275
100 books for $500

_____
_____
_____
_____
_____
_____
_____
_____
_____
_____
_____
_____
_____
_____
_____
_____
_____
_____
_____
_____
_____
_____
_____
_____
_____
_____
_____

About the Author

Diana Robinson *became* a mother in 1996; a wife in 2008; a minister in 2010; an author, grandmother, and Bible-based radio program, *Make Your Day Count,* cohost in 2019; and a business owner in 2020 – Transformed Publishing.

In Christ we *become.* We grow into each life-role and continue to develop.

As of January 2024, Transformed Publishing has produced and published twenty-three authors and a total of forty-two books. Never despise small beginnings.

> The end of a thing is better than its beginning; the patient in spirit is better than the proud in spirit.

-Ecclesiastes 7:8

Letting it happen through an act of obedience, a leap of faith, practicing and perfecting gifts, talents, and purpose has produced evidence that continues to glorify God and will outlive my natural years of life. We each have unique assignments. Remember, to let *yours* happen!

Let it Happen.

Visit www.transformedpublishing.com

More Books by Diana Robinson

Once stop link to my Amazon Author Page:

Gaining Strength for Your Journey will help you establish the necessary foundation to anchor your identity and equip you to make your dream a reality.

❖ Have you done all you can to follow God's directions, only to be met with frustrating delays?

❖ Have you ever wondered where God is when it seems like your destiny is deterred?

❖ How will the life God designed for you actually become what you desire?

❖ Will you remain diligent to rise to the level of distinction you were created for?

Gaining Strength for Your Journey will awaken the vision within you to operate confidently in all God has entrusted and packaged within you. The time is now to develop what is right for you.

The *Believer's* **Authority**

How to Overcome
Bible Study Series
Study Guide, Workbook, & Journal
By Diana Robinson

- You are God's Masterpiece.
- You are the Apple of His Eye.
- You are an Expression of the Love of Jesus Christ.
- You were sent by the Lord to the earth for a Divine Purpose.
- You are here to manifest the vision that He wrote about you in the books of heaven before you were even formed in your mother's womb. You have been given authority, power, and access to live a victorious life.

Q: Do you believe this, but need help with unbelief?
A: This Study Guide, Workbook, & Journal is for you!

This Study Guide, Workbook, & Journal is broken down into six sessions. It is recommended that you spend an entire week of devotional time studying, meditating, praying, and journaling on each topic. Additional journaling pages are located in the back of this book.

The Word of God is meant to cleanse, transform, refresh, & renew our minds. Mind transformation is a continuous process that we must do diligently. Ultimately, we must 'lose our mind' and let the mind of Christ root and take dominion in our mind.

A fiction yet factual book series to help overcome the maze of the mind. Book #1: TIED to the negative consequences of a life changing decision made out of fear. Internally DESTROYED by self-sabotage in response to an out-of-control situation. Emotionally & mentally TORMENTED moment by moment as a result of an unescapable tragedy. CONFUSED because when someone doesn't know where they are going, everywhere looks the same.

The *I Lost My Mind* series honestly reveals and confronts unmentionable & unmanageable matters of the mind. We must lose that mind in exchange for the mind of Christ.

Get a glimpse into the minds of this book's featured characters (Tye, Dee, Torie, & Conner). Engaging color interior. Relevant content.

Book #2. Overtly labeled REBELLIOUS and living through the consequences because she took a stand for the truth. The past she escaped ALONE has again become her reality. SKEPTICAL because the plan that sounded good for his family has proven to be neither sound nor good. Attained financial and social prestige, no option is out of his reach and every choice leaves him more DISSATISFIED.

Get a glimpse into the minds of this book's featured characters (Reba, Allie, Skype, & Dyz).

I Write What is Right reinforces daily positive affirmations from A-Z for children. Both Print & Cursive Editions Available.

Say it! Recognize it!
Read it! Write it!
Meditate on it!
Believe it! Be it!

I Write What is Right promotes letter & word recognition; handwriting, spelling, & reading practice; Biblical values; and increases self-esteem. Daily positive affirmations are key to clarity & confidence. You have the mind of Christ.

DIANA ROBINSON
& the Shovlin FAMILY

There are so many great things Papa can do and he does them because he loves me.

From things small to big, Papa is always ready for every gig!

Reach it! Fix it! Drive it! Play it! Teach it! Buy it! Inflate it! Build it! And so much more! PAPA CAN & PAPA WILL!

This book is a great addition to your children's libraries to acknowledge the contributions of each and every Papa to enhance the lives of their loved ones.

Relevant and engaging for children of all ages. Use this book to teach, empower, and talk to your children about making Jesus' PEACE a reality by choosing to be full of joy and love, even when things do not go their way.

Exploring
the Fruits of the Spirit
with Joy

LOVE, PEACE, & JOY
By Diana Robinson